ON ASSIGNMENT

Peering into
Darkness

Rebecca L. Johnson

PICTURE CREDITS
Cover (background), cover (bottom right), pages 1, 2–3, 20 (inset), 20–21, 22 (left), 22 (right), 23, 24–25 (inset), 24–25, 30 Timothy G. Laman/National Geographic Image Collection; cover (bottom left), pages 3, 14, 14–15, 16, 17, 18, 19, 19 (upper right), 26 Stephen Alvarez/National Geographic Image Collection; cover (back), pages 4–5 (inset), pages 12–13 Emory Kristof/National Geographic Image Collection; pages 4–5, 6–7, 8, 10, 11 (left) Stephen Low Company; page 5 Jonathan Blair/National Geographic Image Collection; pages 8–9, 11 (right) Rod Catanach/Woods Hole Oceanographic Institution; pages 12–13 (background) Richard Lutz/Rutgers University; page 13 (upper right) Craig Cary/University of Delaware College of Marine Studies; page 21 (bottom right) Jeffrey L. Rotman/Corbis.

ARTWORK
Linda Kelen

LOCATOR GLOBES
Mapping Specialists Limited

Produced through the worldwide resources of the National Geographic Society, John M.. Fahey, Jr., President and Chief Executive Officer; Gilbert M. Grosvenor, Chairman of the Board; Nina D. Hoffman, Executive Vice President and President, Books and School Publishing.

PREPARED BY NATIONAL GEOGRAPHIC SCHOOL PUBLISHING
Ericka Markman, President; Steve Mico, Vice President, Editorial Director; Marianne Hiland, Editorial Manager; Jim Hiscott, Design Manager; Kristin Hanneman, Illustrations Manager; Matt Wascavage, Manager of Publishing Services; Sean Philpotts, Production Coordinator; Production: Clifton M. Brown III, Manufacturing and Quality Control

PROGRAM DEVELOPMENT
Kate Boehm Jerome

CONSULTANTS/REVIEWERS
Dr. James Shymansky, E. Desmond Lee Professor of Science Education, University of Missouri-St. Louis
Glen Phelan, science writer, Palatine, Illinois

BOOK DEVELOPMENT
Thomas Nieman, Inc.

BOOK DESIGN
Herman Adler Design

Published by the National Geographic Society
1145 17th Street, N.W.
Washington, D.C. 20036-4688

ISBN: 0-7922-8451-8

Third Printing September, 2011.
Printed in Canada

A lizard clings tightly to a branch in a rain forest at night.

Contents

Inside a cave far underground

Light reveals clusters of giant tube worms that live in darkness on the sea floor.

Introduction

One Mile Down

A small submarine called *Alvin* glides above the sea floor, a mile beneath the surface. Not a single ray of sunlight has ever touched the bottom here. Suddenly, the sub comes upon a strange scene. Giant blood-red tube worms—taller than a person—sprout next to a crack in the sea floor. They are covered with crabs as white as ghosts.

What lurks beyond the reach of the sub's lights? And what lives in other dark and shadowy places on Earth? To discover what's out there, we need tools that can "see" where we cannot.

In this book, you'll go on assignment with scientists who peer into dark places. Some explore the deep sea. Others crawl through caves far underground. Still others roam through forests at night. Armed with special lights and cameras, these people see what has long been hidden from our eyes. Get set to view what few have seen before!

Scientists explore the deep sea in the small submarine *Alvin*.

5

Hot Spots in a Cold Sea

Hot, chemical-rich water gushes from a
hydrothermal vent on the ocean floor.
These images were captured by an
IMAX camera for a giant-screen film.

Water spurts from cracks in the sea floor. It is fiercely hot and full of poisonous chemicals. Welcome to a hydrothermal vent, an island of warmth on the cold ocean bottom. Giant tube worms and many other creatures live together here in total darkness.

Atlantic Ocean

Galápagos Islands

South America

Pacific Ocean

Hydrothermal vents first discovered

The first **hydrothermal vent** was discovered in 1977 by scientists exploring the sea floor in *Alvin*. Since then, more vents have been found in other parts of the ocean.

Hydrothermal vents occur in very deep water—on average, about 2100 meters (6900 feet) down. Most vents lie along mid-ocean ridges. These are places where some of the huge plates of Earth's crust come together.

At first, scientists didn't understand how a whole **community** of organisms could live in complete darkness at the bottom of the sea. Elsewhere on Earth, sunlight is the source of energy for life. Plants and **algae** use this light to produce food. These producers, in turn, are eaten by animals.

Over time, scientists figured out that the source of energy for vent communities comes from chemicals, not light. Tiny life forms called **bacteria** live in the water around the vents. These bacteria break down chemicals in the hot water. As they do, energy is released. The bacteria use this energy to make food. The bacteria, in turn, are food for other vent creatures.

Fun Facts! The process of making food from light energy is called *photosynthesis*. Making food from chemicals, in the absence of light, is called *chemosynthesis*.

Changing Views of Vents

Diving down to a deep-sea vent in a submarine is dangerous and expensive. That's why people want to learn as much as they can on every dive. Researchers can't leave the sub. The water pressure outside would crush them. So they use the sub's mechanical arms to collect rocks, water samples, and a few small animals.

Probably the best tool for studying life around the vents is a camera. Early pictures of vents were taken with ordinary video cameras mounted on the sub. But those pictures weren't very clear.

So researchers kept improving their lights and cameras. The *Alvin* was fit with new cameras. One was the type used to make IMAX films. IMAX pictures of vent animals are remarkably clear. The smallest details of their bodies are easy to see.

These details mean a lot to scientists. Stephen Low, the director of the IMAX deep-sea filming project, has played an important part in developing this film. IMAX film is now a key tool for learning about life in the deep sea.

Alvin **cruises toward its research site.**

Scientist Richard Lutz (left) and filmmaker Stephen Low (right) are leading the filming expedition at the bottom of the ocean.

If giant tube worms have no mouths, how do bacteria get into their bodies? Scientists discovered that very young tube worms do have mouths and stomachs. Bacteria can get in. But as the worms grow, these body parts disappear. The bacteria end up trapped inside the worms.

Pale crabs and weird fish live among tube worms in the vent community.

What the Cameras Reveal

So, what have scientists learned from their pictures? In older photographs, scientists saw lots of tiny specks in the water around the vents. They took new pictures using a camera with a special magnifying lens. These close-ups revealed that the millions of specks were actually flea-sized animals called *amphipods*.

In other pictures, scientists studied tangled clumps of what looked like string. The "string" turned out to be soft-bodied spaghetti worms.

On rocks around the vents, giant clams sit like clusters of huge grapes. Dark red shrimp with glowing eyes clamber over them. Long, eel-like fish slither among the worms.

Tube worms are the largest ventdwellers. Standing up to 3 meters (almost 10 feet) tall, they look like giant tubes of lipstick. They have no mouths, no eyes, and no stomachs. How do they survive? Countless numbers of bacteria live inside the worms. Through chemosynthesis, these bacteria make food for themselves *and* the worms. The worms shelter the bacteria and get all their meals in return!

A red shrimp perches on giant clams.

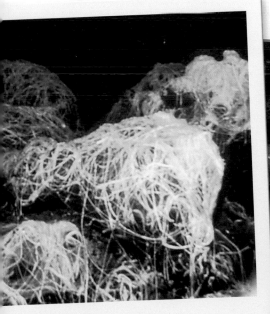

Spaghetti worms

Bring on the Heat

Alvin researchers used special tools to take the temperature of water in different places around a vent. In doing this, they discovered a strange-looking worm called a Pompeii worm. This worm can stand hotter temperatures than any other living thing on Earth.

Pompeii worms can survive in extreme heat.

Pompeii worms are about as long and thick as a person's finger. They live inside tubes that they build on rocks right at the edge of a vent. Scientists used to think that nothing could live in temperatures above 54° C (130° F). But Pompeii worms proved them wrong. Craig Cary is a **biologist** from the University of Delaware. He found that these little worms can survive temperatures up to 80° C (176° F). That's close to boiling!

High-tech cameras reveal new details about life around deep-sea vents. More than 25 years after discovering the vents, scientists are still finding new life forms. And they are just starting to understand how these creatures live together so far beneath the waves.

A Pompeii worm, out of its tube

Alvin's arm reaches toward amphipods, fish, and tube worms to help scientists record life at the bottom of the ocean.

Hidden Passageways in Earth

Deep underground, the scientists struggle through a narrow passage. It's a tight squeeze between walls of jagged rock. At last they step out into a huge room. It's so big that the beams from their flashlights don't light up the other end.

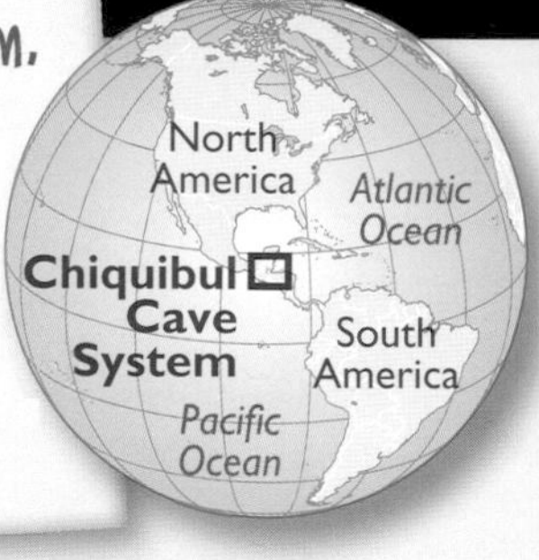

North America
Atlantic Ocean
Chiquibul □
Cave
System
South America
Pacific Ocean

Without their flashlights, of course, the team would see nothing at all. The darkness inside a cave is as black as the deep ocean floor.

Where is this science team? They are hundreds of meters below ground in Central America.

Towering rock formations in Chiquibul cave

The Chiquibul River carved out this cave.

They squeeze and scramble through the Chiquibul (CHEE kwee bull) cave. The cave was formed by the Chiquibul River. It flows across Belize and Guatemala on its way to the Caribbean Sea. Along part of its course, the river flows underground. Over thousands of years, it has carved the cave from solid rock.

Thomas Miller, a **geologist** from the University of Puerto Rico, found part of the cave in 1982.

Since then he's been back many times to explore it. So far, he and his teams have found four giant underground rooms, or **caverns**. They've mapped many kilometers of passageways.

In 1998, Thomas's team tried to follow a passageway they thought might connect two large caverns. But swirling river waters blocked their path. So a year later, they came back—with diving gear.

Preparing for the Challenge

The team numbered 14 people in all. To reach the Chiquibul cave, they hiked for days through dense rain forest. Helicopters airlifted in many of their supplies. They brought freeze-dried food, scuba-diving equipment, and lots of cave-exploring equipment. Stephen Alvarez, a photographer for the National Geographic Society, went along.

The team split into two groups and headed underground. Each group set up a camp in one of the caverns. Can you imagine camping underground? It sounds cold and damp. In fact, the cave was pretty warm—a constant 23° C (74° F). But the team could tell only by their watches whether it was day or night.

After the camps were set up, it was time to explore. In one cavern, expert cave diver James Brown put on dive gear and armed himself with underwater flashlights. Then he slipped into the cold, inky waters of the flooded passageway. As he swam, he played out a white nylon cord. It was his lifeline back to safety.

Thomas and the others waited at the spot where James had disappeared. Ninety minutes ticked by. Then in a rush of bubbles, James surfaced. He had good news! The passageway led to the other cavern. That meant Chiquibul is a single cave. And it is over 40 kilometers (25 miles) long—the longest known cave in Central America.

Cool Fix! On the way to their campsites, the teams had to wade through chest-deep water. To keep food and other supplies dry, they inflated car-tire inner tubes. Instant rafts! They piled the gear on top.

Diving into dark water is the only way to explore the flooded passageways of Chiquibul cave.

Members of the team cross the underground Chiquibul River as they explore the cave.

Hidden Treasures

The team made other discoveries deep in the cave. They found thousands of bat skeletons. Some were more than 10,000 years old. The skeletons were from several different kinds of bats. One type—a large vampire bat—is now **extinct**.

Jean Krejca was the team's biologist. In still, slimy pools, she took samples of unusual bacteria. She also found a rare cave crab and a cave shrimp with no eyes.

In other parts of the cave, the team found large clay pots and stones for grinding corn.

Team **archeologist** Logan McNatt believes these objects were left behind by ancient Mayan people. The Maya lived in this area more than 1000 years ago. They probably came into the cave to get water and honor their gods. Maybe some of them liked to explore dark passageways, too.

Scientists think that the Chiquibul cave began to form about 800,000 years ago. As long as its river keeps flowing, the cave will keep growing and changing. And researchers like Thomas Miller will keep coming back. Who knows what secrets still lie hidden in this damp darkness?

Jean Krejca and Taco van Ieperen take samples from the water to learn what's living in the cave's river.

Mayan plate
found in the
Chiquibul cave

Ancient Maya left pottery
in the cave long ago.

Chapter 3

Eyes in the Night

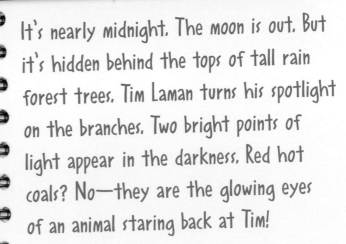

Tim Laman takes a photo in the dark forest.

It's nearly midnight. The moon is out. But it's hidden behind the tops of tall rain forest trees. Tim Laman turns his spotlight on the branches. Two bright points of light appear in the darkness. Red hot coals? No—they are the glowing eyes of an animal staring back at Tim!

A Malay civet searches for food at night.

Tim Laman loves to explore forests at night. With cameras, spotlights, and **night-vision goggles**, he wanders through the darkness. He is in search of animals that few people ever see. He's out to capture these **nocturnal** creatures on film for National Geographic.

Nocturnal animals sleep during the day but are active at night. When the sun sets, these forest dwellers emerge from dens and tree holes and other hiding places. All night long they scramble and glide through a world of shadows. They search for food, find mates, and care for their young. When the sun rises, they retreat to their hiding places.

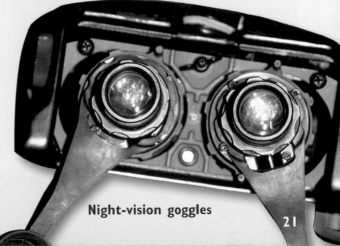

Night-vision goggles

Have Lights, Will Travel

Tropical rain forests are home to a huge variety of animals. Scientists know very little about most of them, especially those that come out at night. Tim has spent hundreds of nights finding and photographing these creatures in southeast Asia, Indonesia, and Malaysia.

How does Tim find his subjects? Often, he'll walk quietly through the forest, shining spotlights into the treetops. Many nocturnal animals have eyes that reflect light. Their eyes "glow" in the glare of a spotlight.

Tim sometimes uses his goggles and **night-vision scopes**. These devices make the faintest glimmer of light appear brighter. With them, Tim can see trees and rocks and other objects in a forest, even on the darkest nights.

Brown owl

Flying bat

Sometimes Tim uses ropes to pull himself into the treetops. Hanging in midair, he's come face to face with sharp-clawed owls. Owls can see very well in the dark. But they rely mostly on their sense of hearing to hunt and catch mice, lizards, and frogs at night. Can't see the owl's ears? They are on either side of its head, hidden under feathers!

Tim often sees tarsiers in the treetops at night. These big-eyed insect eaters can see well in the dark. With their huge ears, they can hear the faintest sounds, too.

Snakes, on the other hand, have poor eyesight. But they can feel tiny movements, or vibrations. They also have a keen sense of smell. Many rain forest snakes hunt frogs and sleeping birds at night.

A tarsier peers at Tim from out of the darkness.

23

Super Senses

Some of the best-known night hunters are bats. One night in Indonesia, just after sunset, Tim was sitting on the side of a cliff. He gazed at the forest below. All of a sudden, he heard the whirring of 10,000 pairs of wings. Overhead, the sky filled with bats. They were streaming out of a cave, heading to the forest to eat moths and other insects.

On another night in the forest, Tim stopped and turned off his headlamp. As his eyes grew used to the dark, he spotted a starworm covered with glowing green spots! Why does the starworm produce its own light? That's a mystery scientists are trying to solve.

By capturing night creatures on film, Tim Laman helps us learn about rain forest animals we know little about. Worldwide, rain forests are at risk. Huge numbers of trees are being cut and the land cleared for farming. As rain forests disappear, so do the animals in them. The more we can learn about rain forest creatures, the better our chances of saving them and their forest homes.

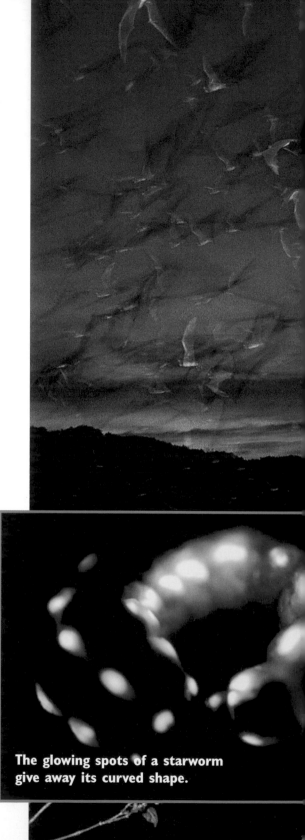

The glowing spots of a starworm give away its curved shape.

Thousands of bats
leave a cave at sunset
to search for food.

Solving Everyday Problems

Imagine crawling through a narrow passageway deep underground. You need a flashlight to see where you are going. But you also need to have both hands free as you squeeze between the rocks. How do you solve this problem? Cave researchers like those on Thomas Miller's Chiquibul team solved it by using headlamps. A headlamp is really just a flashlight worn on your head. It's a clever solution for bringing a light into the darkness—a light you don't have to hold on to.

Headlamps help light up the darkness of a cave.

Whether you're exploring a cave or just having another busy weekend, problems are a part of life. Solving everyday problems can be tough. But it can also be fun. And by following a few simple steps, you can become a pro at problem solving. Let's check it out!

Think Tank

Step 1 — Identify the Problem

Problems can pop up any time, anywhere. When they do, the secret is not to sweat it but to solve it. The first step to solving a problem is to stop and figure out exactly what the problem is.

How Can I Balance the Bag?

Your mother asks you to go to the grocery store to get a few things for dinner. One of them happens to be ice cream! You jump on your scooter and zoom off to the store. After getting everything on the list, you go through the checkout. Your purchases are all put in a single plastic grocery bag.

Once outside, you realize you have a problem. Your bag of groceries is heavy. Carrying the bag in one hand is going to make you very unbalanced on your scooter. How are you going to carry it in a safe way?

Step 2 — Brainstorm Solutions

Problems are challenges. But even the toughest ones have solutions. To find them, you need to be creative. The second step in problem solving is to brainstorm possible solutions. Brainstorming gets those little gray cells working. Look at the problem from different angles. Think of as many possible solutions as you can. And remember—at this stage, nothing is a dumb idea!

What Options Do I Have?

You sit down on the curb to think. You make a mental list of possible solutions to your problem. Maybe you could:

- *walk home, carrying the groceries in one hand and pushing your scooter.*

- *leave the groceries at the checkout, scoot home, and come back on your bike, which has a rack for carrying stuff.*

- *put some of the groceries in another bag from the store. Then you could slip one bag over each of the scooter's handles for balance.*

- *strap the bag to your body somehow, so you'd be balanced and your hands would be free to steer the scooter.*

27

Step 3 Evaluate Solutions

The next step in problem solving is to decide which one of your possible solutions is the best. Some solutions won't work for different reasons. But in the list there may be a gem of an idea that you can expand into a workable solution.

This Idea Might Just Work . . .

You go over your mental list. Walking home will take a long time—the ice cream will melt. Going and getting your bike seems too complicated. Having two bags will allow you to be balanced on your scooter, but it'll still be pretty awkward, and the bags might interfere with steering.

If only you had a backpack. Hey, wait a minute . . . if you could wear the grocery bag like a backpack, the weight of the groceries would be centered on your back. Your hands would be free, and you'd be balanced!

Step 4 Choose a Solution and Implement It

The final step in problem solving is to choose what seems to be the best solution and give it a try. If it doesn't work right off the bat, simply trying it may lead to a better solution. Keep thinking and keep at it. Before you know it, your problem will be solved.

. . . And It Does!

You study the plastic grocery bag. It's got two handles. A backpack has two shoulder straps. What if you slipped your arms through the bag's handles, just as you would with a backpack?

You give it a try, and it works—instant backpack. You're balanced and back on your scooter. Problem solved! And, boy, is that ice cream ever going to taste great for dessert!

Problem Solving on Your Own

Here's the Problem

It's late on a stormy night. You're talking to your best friend on your mom's cell phone when suddenly the lights go out. You tell your friend you'll call her back. You push the "end call" button on the phone. For a few seconds, the key pad gives off an eerie glow. When it goes dark, you're surrounded by inky blackness.

You need to get downstairs to find out why the lights went out. But you don't have a flashlight, or even a candle, to help light your way. And since your room is a mess, you're afraid you are going to trip over something if you try to walk across your room in the dark! What are you going to do?

Find a Solution

Work with a small group to discuss what you might do. Use the steps below to guide your thinking.

1 Identify the Problem
2 Brainstorm Solutions
3 Evaluate Solutions

Be creative when brainstorming ideas as you figure out a way to solve this problem.

Science Notebook

Fun Facts

• Night is the safest time for many animals to move around. They are less likely to be seen by predators.

• The mid-ocean ridge system—where most deep-sea hydrothermal vents occur—covers about 75,000 kilometers (46,600 miles). It circles the globe. Most of it has not been explored.

• Scientists have mapped roughly 64 kilometers (40 miles) of passageways and caverns in Chiquibul cave. They think there are at least another 32 kilometers (20 miles) waiting to be discovered.

Web Connection

You can explore all sorts of dark places on the Internet, without ever leaving home! If reading about hydrothermal vents makes you long to "go deep," try visiting www.nationalgeographic.com/ngm/0010 and www.ocean.udel.edu/expeditions.

For a closer look at the Chiquibul cave, head to www.nationalgeographic.com/chiquibul.

Or if peering into the shadows of a rain forest at night sounds more like how you'd like to spend your time, visit www.nationalgeographic.com/ngm/0110.

Take the Challenge!

Pick a dark place you'd like to explore. Write a one-page explanation of how you'd explore that place and what you'd need to do it. What would you expect to find? Share your imaginary journey with your classmates.

Photographer Tim Laman at work in the trees

Glossary

algae plantlike forms that usually live in water and make food using light energy

archeologist person who studies the remains of civilizations, including skeletons, buildings, and objects made by people

bacteria microscopic, single-celled life forms

biologist person who studies living things

cavern very large underground room that is part of a cave

community collection of different kinds of organisms living together in one place

extinct no longer living on Earth

geologist person who studies rocks

hydrothermal vent crack in Earth's crust from which hot water gushes. These vents form around "seams" between plates of the crust. Melted rock lies below the seams and heats the water.

night-vision goggles special eyewear that makes it possible to see in the dark

night-vision scope instrument similar to a telescope that makes it possible to see in very dim light

nocturnal awake and active at night

Index